Original title:
A Cactus Called Patience

Copyright © 2025 Creative Arts Management OÜ
All rights reserved.

Author: Robert Ashford
ISBN HARDBACK: 978-1-80581-763-5
ISBN PAPERBACK: 978-1-80581-290-6
ISBN EBOOK: 978-1-80581-763-5

Chronicles of the Tenacious

In a desert so dry, with a grin quite wide,
Stands a hero who waits, and takes it in stride.
With arms open wide, it invites the sun,
And laughs at the storms, thinking this is fun!

His friends all complain, they need water, they plead,
But he sits there with glee, on a throne made of seed.
A sip here and there? Oh, that's just too plain!
He's got patience down to an art; what a gain!

When a bird lands to peck, he just twirls and winks,
"Good luck, feathered friend, this is not what you think!"
Prickly and proud, he has quite the charm,
Says, "With time on my side, I can't come to harm!"

So raise up a glass to the spines and the cheer,
To the one who can flourish while others just fear.
In his world of green laughter, oh what a sight,
He teaches us patience can also mean light!

Of Shadows and Light

In a world full of rush, he says, "Take a seat!
Why rush when you can just use your own feet?"
With shadows so long, he grins wide and bright,
"I'm thriving on stillness, now isn't that right?"

When the sun starts to rise, he yawns oh so grand,
"Morning, dear sunlight, come hold out your hand!"
But if rain should arrive, he just giggles with glee,
"Watch me dance in the droplets; come join my spree!"

His spikes are his armor, he's sharp and so sly,
"Why blend with the crowd? I just aim for the sky!"
He loves the attention, the curious gaze,
"Come closer, my dear, there's no need to be fazed!"

So here's to that fellow with patience so rare,
Though prickly and tough, he's truly quite rare.
He shows us that joy can grow tall in the night,
In shadows and light, all are welcome to bite!

Petals in the Parched

In a land where raindrops flee,
Petals laugh at drought's decree.
'Tis a game of grow and stall,
Who needs water, after all?

Spines are armor, soft in jest,
Belly laughs from nature's chest.
Dance in dust, they sing their tune,
'Our party starts at noon!'

Green Against the Grit

In the desert's endless bake,
Green warriors stand, no mistake.
With grit and giggles, they parade,
Laughing at the sun's tirade.

Twisting tales of sun and sand,
Fierce and friendly, they take a stand.
A slouchy walk, a bounce, a cheer,
'Don't mind us, we thrive right here!'

Seasons of Solitude

Beneath the sun, all alone,
Cracks in earth feel like home.
Each season brings a punchline new,
The desert's wit, it grows and grew.

Spring is for the blooms that tease,
Winter's jokes, just frigid breeze.
Through the drought, they jest and jibe,
Who needs friends? We've got our vibe!

The Tenacity of Thorns

Thorns that poke with playful glee,
'Come get comfy right next to me!'
Meeting faces with a grin,
'Don't be shy, just dive right in!'

With every prick, a laugh in tow,
Smiles bloom beneath the woe.
They stand strong, though dry and bare,
In this spiny love affair!

Clinging to Tomorrow

Well, here I sit, I'm not a chair,
Spines on my back, but never despair.
I dream of sunshine, I dream of rain,
Waiting for folks to feel my pain.

Oh, I see them rush, I see them fret,
While I just chill, no big regret.
In every prick, a story unfolds,
Of dreams that sparkle like treasures of gold.

Nature's Quiet Rebellion

The garden's alive with buzzing intrigue,
While I'm the oddball, just looking fatigued.
With blooms of courage but prickly wit,
I cheer for the daisies, all gorgeous and fit.

They dance in the breeze, a floral parade,
While I stand still, no plans to invade.
Yet, I smile wide, don't need their flair,
For my silent charm is beyond compare.

Tenacity in the Heat

The sun blazes down, and I don't sweat,
Just sip on sunlight, no fear, no fret.
While others wilt, I'm strong as can be,
Like a sitcom star, quirky and free.

Each day a joke, I take in stride,
With roots so strong, I cannot hide.
I wear my quirks with unabashed pride,
In the heat of the day, I don't need to hide.

Waiting for the Rain

Clouds roll in, I strike a pose,
Petals wide open, like a showbiz rose.
Though I'm a skeptical little spire,
I'm waiting for blessings, full of desire.

The raindrops laugh, they tease and play,
While I stand here, hoping they'll stay.
In the rain's embrace, I'd dance with glee,
But for now, it's just me, myself, and my tea.

Embracing the Scorch

Sunshine is my buddy,
But sweat is my right hand,
I smile in the heat,
While my skin makes a stand.

My friends, they all wither,
They look at me, confused,
I thrive in this chaos,
While they cling to the used.

Water? Not for me,
I sip the sun's sweet brew,
Laughing at the rivers,
While the others feel blue.

Heat waves dance around,
I wear my prickles with pride,
In this blazing party,
I'm a quirky cactus guide.

Life in the Toughest Terrain

Bumping along rough paths,
With a smile made of spikes,
I dodge all the troubles,
And avoid the hobo bikes.

Others cry and complain,
As they trip on the ground,
But I stand strong and tall,
In my sandy playground.

Sunburns? What are those?
I'll take them and cheer,
While they grumble and moan,
I'm the cactus of cheer!

Every tumble I take,
Is a dance with my fate,
I shimmy through the dirt,
In this wild desert state.

Silence of the Succulent

In a world so loud,
I embrace the soft hush,
While others shout for water,
I giggle and just brush.

Oh, they fuss over mist,
And fret about their shade,
But in my prickly kingdom,
Life's a different parade.

I wiggle in the breeze,
With joy on my spiked face,
While they sip and complain,
I groove in my own space.

The desert sings a tune,
While my friends dance and tire,
I sit in my stillness,
Fueling my own fire.

Roots Deep in Harshness

In the driest of soils,
My roots go ten feet down,
While others flinch and panic,
I wear my spiky crown.

Tough love from the ground,
It's a rugged embrace,
I thrive on this madness,
While others flee the race.

With every stormy gust,
I just sway with the winds,
Giggling at the chaos,
As the funny life begins.

While they dream of rain,
I laugh in the bright sun,
For in my thorny heart,
This sunshine's just begun.

Silence Sings of Survival

In the desert, I quietly thrive,
A spiky friend, still alive.
Sun beats down, my humor's bright,
I wear my pain with pure delight.

Water's scarce, but life is grand,
I dance alone, no hand in hand.
Rumbles in the sand bring glee,
To be a prickly soul, that's me!

Neighbors laugh, they flee in fright,
Yet here I stand, a comical sight.
I chuckle soft, while birds take flight,
In my own world, I am a knight.

Roots run deep, my spirit soars,
In arid lands, I've opened doors.
Surprises bloom, my heart's a song,
In quiet strength, I still belong.

Faith in the Fertile

Even rocks know how to sprout,
In tough terrain, I find my route.
With little to share, I hoot and holler,
Life's wild jokes make me laugh louder.

Seeds may trip on stony ground,
Yet friendship's laughter can be found.
In silence, hope begins to play,
Who knew that roots could have such sway?

A wink from sunbeams brings me cheer,
Growth's a party, it's quite clear.
I sway and tease, with not a care,
My prickly charm is beyond compare.

Nurtured by dreams in barren fields,
I stand by faith, the soldier yields.
Through hurdles high, I leap and bound,
In soil of jest, my joys abound.

Yearning in the Yonder

Oh, to stretch beyond this shroud,
To dance with clouds, oh so loud.
But here I sit, with eyes aglow,
Wishing on stars, what a show!

The moonlight bathes my prickly frame,
Each twinkle whispers, 'Play this game.'
Perhaps I'll tumble, joyfully roll,
Into a world that warms my soul.

Despite the heat, I dream so wide,
A jester's heart, I take in stride.
With roots that hold, I giggle still,
For every wish, there's time to fill.

My heart may yearn, but laughter's cure,
In each harsh breeze, I'm feeling sure.
A little spin, a wobbly sway,
Life's a jest, come what may!

Verdant Vows

Through spiny trials, I make a pact,
To joke with fate, that's how I act.
My needles guard, yet laughter's free,
In prickle and play, here's where I'll be.

With every storm, I promise cheer,
Green vows of hope, I hold so dear.
Alongside thorns, my spirit sings,
In arid lands, joy truly springs.

The sun may blaze, but I stay bright,
In shadows cast, I find the light.
A quirky life is still my vow,
To wear a grin, I'll show you how.

Spiky comrade, come take my hand,
In this dry joke, we'll take a stand.
Together we'll laugh, not run to hide,
In verdant grace, let's twist and glide.

Thorns and Time

In a garden so bright and wide,
Lives a plant with a prickly side.
It waits for the sun, it waits for the rain,
With a smile on its face, despite the pain.

Every kid and dog gives it a poke,
"Oh look, it's the plant that's always a joke!"
But the wise old sage with the red cowboy hat,
Says patience is key, just look at that!

Resilience in the Desert

In a desert that's hot, oh what a scene,
Lives a spiny friend, with a heart so keen.
While others are melting, losing their sway,
It stands tall and proud, come what may.

It giggles at rain that's nowhere in sight,
Winks at the clouds, "You'll get here tonight!"
With a jolly good laugh and a poke to the sky,
It knows that good things take time to apply.

The Slow Bloom

With petals all curled, it starts to pretend,
"I'm hiding," it says, "just until spring's end."
It tickles the earth with its tiny green toes,
Then pops out a bloom—well, that's how it goes!

While flowers rush by, all flashy and bright,
This little dude smiles, "I'll get it right!"
With a pinch and a poke, here comes the grand show,
It's worth every second, just watch it glow!

Prickly Endurance

In the land of the saguaros, tall and grand,
Stands one little guy, with quite the demand.
"Why hurry, oh why? What's the rush all about?"
With thorns all around, it jeers with a shout.

It laughs at the raindrops, "You'll come when you can,
While I sip on my dreams, I'll make my own plan!"
So here's to the slow, with their quirky good cheer,
In the dance of endurance, they're the ones we hold dear!

The Thirst for Tomorrow

In the desert's grasp, he stands tall,
Waiting for rain, or just a squall.
His friends the cacti laugh and cheer,
"Come on, dear buddy, it's just a year!"

His spines like needles, but heart so soft,
Dreaming of water, floating aloft.
A sip of dew, he's hoping for bliss,
Yet all he gets is a dry cactus kiss.

The clouds roll by, playing hide and seek,
With every drop he gives a squeak.
A prayer for storms, oh what a plot,
But leaky umbrellas? He's got a lot!

So here's to tomorrow, the horizon so wide,
While our friend waits with his prickly pride.
With laughter around, he takes in the sun,
For the thirst for tomorrow is all in good fun!

Unfurling in Adversity

In a land where sunlight burns the ground,
Our hero waits without a sound.
He stretches his arms, trying to dance,
Waving his spines in a stubborn prance.

His neighbors bloom, so bright and bold,
While he's stuck with stories untold.
"With every battle, I grow a few thorns,"
He chuckles while wearing his thorny horns.

The wind wails a tune, but he's not fazed,
With a laugh he says, "I've been underdazed!"
Patience is key, or so they say,
For every struggle, there's humor at play.

While other plants flaunt their petals and flair,
He stands with pride, without a care.
A poke here and there, he'll never concede,
Unfurling in adversity is quite the creed!

Sanctuary of the Succulent

In a wild garden full of blooms,
Our spiky hero hides from glooms.
His friends are plush, with petals so neat,
While he's just trying to find a little seat.

"Here's my cozy spot, all dry and great!"
He says with a grin, "I'll always wait.
Bring on the weeds, bring on the fuss,
In my sanctuary, it's just me and us!"

With a twist and a turn, he shakes off the dust,
Enjoying his solitude, it's a must.
The wind whispers secrets, the sun gives a wink,
In this quirky place, he starts to think.

So if life gets thorny and things go awry,
Join our spiky friend under the vast sky.
For in this refuge of grooves and crows,
The sanctuary of the succulent is where laughter grows!

The Dance of Drought

When the sun is blazing, the ground's like stone,
Our prickly pal feels quite alone.
But wait! It's a party, not just a drought,
Let's shimmy and shake, let's twist it out!

With his spiny limbs, he bops left and right,
Even in dryness, he keeps it light.
"Why cry for rain when you can boogie?"
He twirls in sand, feeling quite groovy.

The moon takes note, a dance in the night,
While critters gather 'round for the sight.
A little sore from the moves he's made,
He laughs, saying, "Who needs a charade?"

So here's to the drought, to the dance we dare,
With laughter and spines, we make quite the pair.
In every dry spell, there's a chance to prance,
For our friend's got rhythm, and life's a dance!

Melodies of the Sun-Baked

In a garden basking bright,
Laughter tickles the warm air,
A prickly friend with charm,
Whispers secrets without a care.

It wobbles with every breeze,
Swaying to a funky beat,
Wishing for a dance partner,
But all that's there is heat!

A sunhat rests upon its head,
Straws and shades, a fashion show,
Twirling in its sandy bed,
In style, it steals the show!

Oh, but don't get too close,
Those spikes can lead to tears,
But in laughter, we can boast,
Patience grows through the years.

The Stillness of Strength

Standing tall with pride and grace,
Not a worry in this place,
With green arms wide and bright,
It's the life of our delight.

Silent guardian of the land,
Unmoved by storms or shifting sand,
But in its heart, a tiny jest,
A chuckle hidden, never stressed.

Its spines might frighten at first glance,
Yet, it beckons all to dance,
With sand as the stage for all to see,
It knows, it's best to simply be!

A laugh ripples through the air,
As breeze and sunlight make a pair,
It stands unwavering and stout,
In patience, it holds a cheerful route.

Archetype of the Arid

In the desert's hearty glow,
Life's great trickster, we bestow,
With twirls of dust and playful cheer,
Admiring all who wander near.

Golden sun, its trusty friend,
Together, they make time suspend,
With every shadow cast anew,
Bringing smiles from the sky so blue!

But don't be fooled by its tough face,
For laughter hides in this warm space,
A gentle poke, a little tease,
Strength and humor blend with ease.

In the stillness, stories weave,
Of sunshine, laughter, and reprieve,
It knows that life's an artful game,
Where patience is the wildest claim.

Colors of Calm

With hues of green, a joyful sight,
Chilling under stars at night,
Beneath the moon's soft, silver light,
Our cactus twinkles, what a fright!

It pulls the colors from the sky,
Brushes strokes, oh my, oh my,
With every breeze, it bolds its tune,
A masterwork beneath the moon!

Sometimes a flower blooms so bright,
With silly hats, it starts a fight,
In the stillness, blooms take their chance,
To dance their dance, a happy prance.

So let's toast to this quirky sage,
With laughter and calm upon the stage,
In patience, it finds its way to rise,
Living life through funny skies.

Waiting for Rain

In the desert sun, I stand so still,
My hopes for rain, they climb the hill.
With every cloud that floats on by,
I wave my arms and shout, "Oh my!"

The birds just laugh, the locusts cheer,
They tickle my prickles, oh dear, oh dear!
I'm the king of dry, with water dreams,
But here I sit, or so it seems.

Echoes in the Arid Land

I hear a drip, could it be fate?
But no, just friends who talk and skate.
The tumbleweed rolls, a dusty ball,
While I just grin and stand quite tall.

My neighbors whisper, 'Is he alive?'
I nod my head, and they all thrive.
Echoes of laughter swirl around,
In this dry land, joy can be found.

Standing Tall in Dryness

With spines so sharp and wit so keen,
I strut my stuff, the desert queen.
No drops to sip, but hey, that's fine,
I'll toast with shadows, I'm divine!

The sun may dance, the heat may hiss,
But in my heart, there's blissful bliss.
I may be prickly, yes indeed,
But laughter's on my thirstful feed.

Nature's Quiet Tenacity

In the midst of sand, I make my stand,
A quirky figure in a dry, vast land.
With stubborn roots and a cheeky grin,
I pretend to thrive, let the fun begin!

The plants around me are all quite meek,
But I'm the star of this dry creek.
With a wink at fate and a cynical laugh,
I offer the sun my best autograph.

Perpetual Sunrises

Each morning's like a rerun show,
Same bright light, same dusty glow.
Patience waits like a traffic cone,
While sunbeams dance on the windblown stone.

Beneath the sun, it stands so still,
Ignoring all but nature's will.
It's happy just to soak and smile,
Secretly judging us, all the while.

If only we could take its cue,
To sip on sun and just be blue.
Instead, we race and sweat and fret,
While Patience waves, "I'm not upset!"

So embrace the sun's delightful tease,
Relax like Patience in the breeze.
With every dawn, a giggle slight,
Life's a joke, and it's all alright!

The Loneliness of Green

In the desert, he stands so bright,
Sporting spikes with all his might.
But every friend, they pass him by,
Too busy to even say hi.

He leans on solitude, quite spry,
Wonders if it's worth a try.
Looking fabulous, though alone,
His roots whisper, "Just hold the phone."

Oh, the irony of his stance,
While others race, he takes his chance.
"Hello there!" he might just say,
If folks would only slow down and play.

But here he stands, a prickly king,
In the desert, he finds his zing.
Laughs at life, it's all a game,
Loneliness can be quite the fame!

Secrets of Persistence

In the sun, with cacti grace,
Patience smiles, no hint of race.
Gossip flows among the sands,
About the ones who takes their stands.

"Why hurry?" he mumbles soft,
"Just relax, let the world aloft."
He's got wisdom in every thorn,
While sprinters rush, all worn and torn.

The secret sauce? It's slow and steady,
Patience laughs, "You're not ready!"
In his world of sun and heat,
He blooms with laughter, can't take defeat.

A sage among the dust and dreams,
Whispering to all, "Join my teams.
Let's take a moment, yes, just one,
To appreciate the setting sun."

Dunes of Determination

He trudges forth through sandy waves,
Determined to be all that he caves.
With a smile that could light the way,
He laughs as others fail to stay.

"Wanna race?" a mirage teases,
But Patience knows, life's not a breeze.
With roots that dig deep, he holds tight,
"I'll win this race without a fight."

Look at him, proud and tall,
With every sunset, he stands enthralled.
While others fret and rush around,
He knows his worth, sticks to the ground.

So let them go, all mad and fast,
In dunes of time, such fun amassed.
With patience as his trusty steed,
He'll conquer all, take the lead!

Journey of the Thorned

In a desert quite dry, it stood so proud,
With spines like a knight, it shouted loud.
"I'm rough and I'm tough, don't tread on me!"
Oh, the tales it would tell, if only you'd see.

Winds would blow high, it swayed with glee,
Snagging a cactus cat—oh, what a spree!
"You'll stick with me now, a pointy delight!"
Dancing together through the starry night.

It wore a hat made of dust, quite chic,
A fashion statement in the middle of bleak.
Neighbors would laugh, say, "What a sight!"
A punk rocker thriving, all spikily bright.

With sunburnt humor and a twist of fate,
It greeted the sun, wouldn't hesitate.
"Bring on the guests, I won't lose cool!"
Its comical charm, a real desert jewel.

Relics of the Resilient

In the sands of time, it stood alone,
An ancient sage with its spine-like throne.
It whispered to lizards and sang to the sun,
"Life's a prickly dance, let's have some fun!"

Through storms it would rock, a resilient sage,
Chasing its dreams on a sneaky sand page.
"Oh look, here's a raindrop, shall we keep score?"
"One drop's not enough! I demand a bit more!"

With a grin of thorns and a snicker so bright,
It wooed passing critters to join in the fight.
"Gather 'round, friends, let's poke some fun!"
As dust clouds danced 'neath the blazing sun.

With tales of endurance spun in the air,
It wore its proud scars with comical flair.
Relics of the resilient, they say it's true,
That laughter grows best in a garden of blue.

Touching the Sky in Struggles

It reached for the stars, a prickly old dream,
"Higher and higher!" it yelled with a scream.
But clouds came and teased, as it waved its spines,
"Hey, don't rain on my party with those silly lines!"

Pushing through struggles, it wobbled and bent,
"Hey, look at me, I'm a green firmament!"
With each little poke, it laughed in the breeze,
"Sky-high aspirations? I do it with ease!"

The moon giggled softly, a bright silver friend,
As it told its tall tales, laughter didn't end.
"Why reach for the heavens? Look at my form!
I'll stick through it all, I'm a cactus in storm!"

So dare to dream, even if you're a spire,
With humor and grit, you can reach up higher.
Touching the sky while poking fun down,
The world's a big stage, come wear my crown!

The Slow Bloom of Courage

In a world full of rush, it took its sweet time,
"Why bloom today when tomorrow's just fine?"
With patience and laughter, it formed a bright smile,
"I'll wait for the right, it's my favorite style!"

It eyed a kind bloom, so lively and grand,
"Oh, darling, you flaunt, but I'll make my stand!"
With laughter in petals, a grin full of cheer,
"Blooming's an art, let's sip some sweet beer!"

The sun rolled its eyes, a chuckling ball,
"What's taking so long? You're missing the call!"
But wise as it was, it just winked with glee,
"The slow bloom of courage is the best way to be!"

And when it finally burst forth, vibrant and bright,
All the garden erupted in joyful delight.
"See? Timing's everything, I'm just too cool!"
A lesson in humor, right here at the school!

Embracing the Drought

In the desert where the sun blares,
I sip my tea with not a care.
When it rains, I bring the folks a show,
An umbrella – do they really know?

Those thirsty plants can grow quite tall,
While I'm sipping off my wall.
A drought? No problem, I just say,
'It's a diet plan, I'm okay!'

Green envy on my spiky mate,
While I just thrive on sun and fate.
My neighbors think they want a taste,
But in my yard, they'd be misplaced!

Laughter echoes through the dry,
As prickly arms wave up to the sky.
Drought is just a cozy friend,
The fun in waiting never ends!

Vitality in the Void

In barren land, with little cheer,
I strut my stuff, no hint of fear.
For in this void I find my grace,
Behold my roots, a daring chase!

With every poke, a chuckle stored,
A jester proud, my throne, adored.
My friends all frown at lack of rain,
While I just giggle – it's insane!

Water drops, a laughing tease,
Yet here I stand, a sturdy breeze.
My spines, a gate of fuzzy love,
They keep the worries far above!

Amidst the sands, I stand so bright,
With empty pots, I still delight.
Oh, vitality, you're a riot,
In this dry void, I'll start a diet!

The Dance of the Desert

In the land where shadows play,
I twirl and spin and sway away.
With every gust of whirling air,
I am the dance, with prickles flair!

A cactus jig, a pointy groove,
With every twist, I find my move.
While creatures watch and laugh in glee,
'What's that? A dancer, wild and free!'

My spines are partners, come and see,
They poke and prod in harmony.
Together we embrace the heat,
In this dance, we can't be beat!

So join the fun, let laughter flow,
In this dry land, we steal the show.
The desert floor, our waltz and song,
Where every prick is where we belong!

Patience Woven in Spikes

In a garden of slow and steady,
My spiky charm is ever ready.
While others dash and lose their way,
I ponder life, come what may.

A prickly face with wisdom old,
I'm patient, fierce, and never cold.
While friends are rushing off in haste,
I sit with pride, no time to waste!

Each tiny spike, a story told,
About the sun and days of gold.
I watch the world, a wondrous show,
While sipping sunshine, nice and slow.

Patience is my secret spice,
I thrive in dry, you'll pay the price.
So come and join my slow parade,
In this spiky world, I've got it made!

The Art of Endurance

In a pot so small, it stands proud,
A prickly fellow, unbowed.
With little water and bright sun rays,
He cracks a smile most sunny days.

He doesn't fuss, he doesn't fret,
With every drop, he's living yet.
While others wilt and quickly fade,
He waves his arms, a spiky parade!

They call him tough, they call him spiky,
But deep inside, he's just so spiky.
He laughs at storms and heavy rains,
For patience, my friend, he truly gains!

So next time you feel all alone,
Just think of him and his little throne.
With every needle, he sheds a tear,
He grows in style, year after year.

Shadows on Sandy Soil

In a desert bright, he casts a shade,
A proud little figure, a classic charade.
While others shrivel and make a fuss,
He's there chilling, not in a rush.

With sand on his feet and sun on his skin,
He grins at the lizards—let the games begin!
Foes may wither, but he just glows,
A master of waiting, everyone knows.

While the tumbleweeds dance in the breeze,
He just sways back with the greatest of ease.
Each moment is golden, each second is sweet,
He laughs as the world digs in its feet.

So if you find yourself feeling blue,
Think of him and what he can do.
With every shadow, a story will bore,
Of patience and fun—who could want more?

Garden of Grit

In a garden where laughter thrives,
A stout little plant, oh how he drives!
With thorns for armor and roots so bold,
He's a little warrior with tales untold.

He squirts out water, just when it's needed,
While others melt down, he feels unimpeded.
Though winds may howl and sun may blaze,
He takes it all in, in a comical haze.

The flowers gossip and tilt their heads,
They wonder how he sleeps in his beds.
But he just chuckles, with a glance so bright,
"Thank you for the sun, but I'm alright!"

So if you're ever stuck in a rut,
Remember ol' grit with a comical strut.
Embrace the patience, let laughter swell,
In the garden of grit, all will be well.

Emergence from the Dust

From the dusty earth, he peers awake,
With spines like spears, he's ready to take.
A tiny warrior in a world so vast,
He's got jokes for the journey, always a blast.

The winds may howl and the sands may shift,
But every moment, he takes as a gift.
With a wink and a nod, he grows up tall,
A funny little hero, he's loved by all.

Each spring he blossoms, a sight to see,
With colors brightening, it's pure harmony.
He giggles at raindrops, laughs at the sun,
In this landscape of patience, he finds his fun.

So if you feel stuck like a foot in the clay,
Remember the plant who finds a way.
With each little laugh, he blooms just right,
Emerging from dust—what a joyous sight!

The Beauty of Barbs

In the garden, it stands so proud,
Waving its arms, a spiky crowd.
With a smile that's sharp and bright,
Oh, what a sight, what a sight!

Takes its time, can't you see?
Water it once, and it feels free.
Holding onto every drop,
Waiting, laughing, never a stop.

Parents warn, 'Do not touch!'
But those barbs just seem to clutch.
An unexpected prick to the finger,
In its embrace, you might linger.

It dreams of rain with a wink,
While sipping sun, thoughts in sync.
Dancing in the warm wind's jest,
A prickly plant indeed, at best!

Thorns of Time

Once I met a spiky friend,
Who claimed that patience knows no end.
With his thorns, he liked to joke,
'Why rush, dear? Just have a poke!'

For hours he'd sit, soaking rays,
While kids in shorts rushed through their days.
'Oh, what's the hurry?' he'd quip and grin,
'Life's a slow dance, let the fun begin!'

When it rains, he laughs with glee,
Spraying joy, just you and me.
Not one drop he'd dare to waste,
Savoring each in a prickly haste.

But when the sun is high and bright,
He'll gladly bask from day to night.
'Chill out, my friend!' he'd always say,
'Why fret about chores anyway?'

The Desert's Whisper

In the desert, under the sun,
Lives a fellow who loves to pun.
'Why have roots when you can stand?
Barbs are nature's helping hand!'

He chats with lizards, plays peek-a-boo,
While saguaro sings a song so true.
'Water's overrated!' he likes to brag,
'Just check my pals, they're all a snag!'

His philosophy? Just stick around,
Patience in the dust and ground.
'Embrace the drought!' he laughs aloud,
In his spiky heart, he's so proud!

But oh, come night, when stars are bright,
He glimmers just like fairy light.
A desert tale of joy and sprawl,
In his world, there's room for all!

Resilience in the Heat

Meet the one with a prickly heart,
In a world where sunny days start.
He stretches wide, arms in the air,
'Hot and stubborn, but I don't care!'

With every beam that comes his way,
He poses like it's a sun-kissed play.
'Broil away; I'll stay right here!
Everyone loves a good old jeer!'

Kids pass by, they'll stop and stare,
At the tough guy who just doesn't care.
'Take a chance, give a little squeeze,
Join my laughter, if you please!'

He chuckles lightly, all day long,
A nature-given, sunny song.
For he's a spiky soul you see,
With barbed resilience, as free as can be!

Beneath the Harvest Moon

In a garden of dreams, blooms the shy,
With spikes that glimmer, oh my oh my!
It leans to the side, a quirky sight,
Under the moon, it's a silly delight.

A tumble of thoughts in a prickly maze,
Its jokes are sharp in hilarious ways.
Waving its arms like it's having a ball,
It knows how to stand, not to stumble or fall.

With petals that wonder, it's hard to resist,
A master of patience, on life's crazy list.
It nods with a grin, oh what can it say?
"Just chill a bit longer; I'm here to stay!"

So laugh with the weeds, join the fun-filled spree,
No matter how thorny, we'll dance with glee!
For under this moon, in the soft, silver light,
Patience is funny, and surely, it's right!

Shadows of Stubbornness

In the heat of the day, it just won't budge,
With roots in the ground, it won't make a grudge.
It stands with a smile, looking quite proud,
Making fun of the clouds, oh isn't it loud?

With a twist and a turn, it's playing the game,
Of who can be stubborn, who wins the fame?
A dance of the winds, while others just flop,
It's bursting with laughter, not ready to stop.

It wears its green armor, ready for jest,
"Who wants to challenge me? I'm simply the best!"
As neighbors all wilt, it giggles with glee,
"I'm just soaking sunshine, can't you see me?"

So here stands our friend, with a jolly good cheer,
In shadows of stubbornness, it's crystal clear:
That joy comes from patience, no rush, just take heed,
Join the party of life, it's all that you need!

Steadfast Among the Sands

In a land far away, where the dune buggies play,
There's a spiky little fella making its way.
With its arms raised high, it's enjoying the sun,
Creating a ruckus, oh, isn't it fun?

It giggles through storms with a stubborn grin,
"Bring on the challenges, I'm here to win!"
Riding the waves of baked desert air,
It's the king of cool in a godforsaken lair.

The friends of the wind whisper soft "You're bold!"
While dancing with sand, it's a sight to behold.
Its heart beats in rhythm with the sun's golden rays,
Knocking down worries like it's child's play!

So amidst all the chaos, it splashes with flair,
A steadfast buddy, no worries a care.
With laughter it blooms, a wild little blend,
Among sands and sunshine, it's a priceless friend!

A Watchful Life

Through moments that twist, in a cozy embrace,
Stands a chap so watchful, with patience and grace.
With eyes like a hawk, it surveys the land,
Chuckling at chaos, it's all so well-planned.

While friends rush around, in a flurry of motion,
It holds to its ground, like a wise, silly ocean.
"Settle down, everyone, what's all the fuss?"
Life blooms slowly; trust me, don't rush!

With humor aplenty in its prickly facade,
It sprinkles some laughter, a dash of a nod.
Every new day brings fresh stories to weave,
In the garden of time, there's nothing to grieve.

So here it will stand, with a grin ear to ear,
Observing the world, year after year.
With might and with mischief, it chuckles with glee,
In a watchful embrace, oh so quirky and free!

Sunburnt Dreams

In a desert of humor, I lay,
With dreams of palm trees, come what may.
But my sunscreen ran off, oh what a sight,
Now I'm a lobster, much to my fright.

The sun laughed at me, as I turned red,
With visions of shade dancing in my head.
I waved at the cacti, but they just stood tall,
Their prickly forms made me feel quite small.

I asked for a drink, they gave me a joke,
A barrel cactus whispered, 'You need to soak!'
So I sipped on the air, and laughed till I cried,
In this sunburnt dream, I just can't hide.

When evening comes, I'll be a fine roast,
With tales of my folly, I'll proudly boast.
No more sunny dreams, just a shade of despair,
But hey, at least I've got sand in my hair!

Hope Amongst the Thorns

In a garden of prickles, I find my cheer,
With hope shining bright, but the thorns are near.
I tripped on my laughter and fell to the ground,
Among the sharp whispers, my joy can be found.

A squirrel took a dive, right into my plant,
His funny acrobatics made me laugh, I can't!
The thorns tried to sting, but we danced around,
In this quirky arena, good vibes abound.

I wore a big smile, and donned a thick coat,
To navigate through, like a brave little goat.
With laughter like sunlight, we all will survive,
In a world full of thorns, together we thrive.

So here's to the hope in the prickly mess,
With friends by my side, life's a goofy fest!
A joyful salute to the giggles and grins,
In this thorny realm, let the fun begin!

Vows of the Verdant

Beneath the green spikes, we made a pact,
To grow some good humor, that's a fact!
In a ceremony bright, with sunlight and glee,
We vowed to stay silly, just you and me.

The flowers all cheered, but the cacti just poked,
Their sharp little jokes, oh how we all choked!
With vows made of laughter and roots intertwined,
In this verdant affair, joy is well-defined.

As the sun set low, we joined in a dance,
With each prickly poke, we reveled, a chance.
To tickle the spines, and stomp on the ground,
In the vows of the verdant, happiness found.

So here's to the moments that make us alive,
In the garden of giggles, where all of us thrive.
With every sharp jab, a chuckle or two,
In this verdant embrace, life's funny and true!

Surviving the Extremes

In the scorching heat or the icy breeze,
We find our warm laughter, if you please.
With snowflakes and sunburns, we wear a grin,
Through each crazy season, together we spin.

The sun may be hot, and the nights could be cold,
But our funny little stories are worth more than gold.
From cactus to icebergs, we freeze and we sweat,
In this wild little dance, we've not finished yet.

With quips like the wind, and jokes on the rocks,
We navigate life while dodging the shocks.
Through extremes we survive, our spirits intact,
Life's humor a shield, that's a potent fact!

So let's raise a toast with iced tea in the shade,
To the laughter we share, and the fun we've made.
In the heat or the chill, we'll always find seams,
Together forever, surviving extremes!

Nature's Unyielding Heart

In the desert, tall and proud,
Stands a green one, laughing loud.
With arms raised high, it greets the sun,
A prickly friend, just having fun.

Water's scarce, but who needs that?
With a grin, it wears a hat.
Sipping on the morning dew,
It throws a party for the crew.

In a world that seems so dry,
Its sharp wit will never die.
A comedy of spines and glee,
The desert's joke for you and me.

So when life feels harsh and bare,
Remember this green jester there.
Patience shines in oddly ways,
As laughter echoes through its days.

Hope in the Hot Horizons

Beneath the sun, so bold and bright,
A spiky soul shows us delight.
It waves its arms in joyful jest,
A symbol of what patience tests.

When the heat is blazing hot,
This jolly plant has a clever plot.
It dances gently in the breeze,
While keeping cool with utmost ease.

So here it stands, without a care,
Wearily waiting with flair to spare.
Each ribbed arm a tale to tell,
Of waiting games that end quite well.

And in the midst of sand and stone,
A spirit laughs, not all alone.
Hope flourishes in every shade,
In a land where dreams are made.

Joy Amidst the Jagged

In a patch of prickles, oh what joy!
Stand tall like a green-backed toy.
Each jagged edge a punchline found,
A playful heart, with laughter bound.

Friends come to visit, what a sight!
Fearful at first, but soon take flight.
As they share tales, a grin will bloom,
In the company of this spiky room.

The world may seem a dangerous place,
Yet in this garden, there's a safe space.
For laughter grows in the strangest lands,
With joy and patience in its hands.

So let's raise a toast to the green brigade,
With drinks of sunshine, we'll not fade.
Among the sharp, there's room to play,
In the unlikeliest of ways.

The Defiance of Drought

In the heart of a thirsty land,
Stands a figure, tall and grand.
With a wicked grin, it takes a stance,
Outsmarting drought with a funny dance.

Each droplet's a joke, a rarity fine,
This spiky soldier drinks all the wine.
While others wilt in the burning sun,
It thrives on laughs; oh, what fun!

Jumping through the sandy loops,
With roots that dig deep with all its troops.
It challenges fate with a prickly style,
And wears defiance like a smile.

So here's to resilience, sharp and spry,
With humor that will never die.
Embrace the heat, and be like this sage,
Finding joy on life's tough stage.

A Testament of Time

In the desert sun standing tall,
Hoping for rain, but not at all.
With arms outstretched, wearing a grin,
It waits for a shower, patiently thin.

Year after year, it swears it's fine,
To be a thorny friend, a buddy divine.
With a humorous twist, it pokes fun at fate,
Smiling at storms, refusing to wait.

When the clouds finally gather above,
It dances with joy, oh, how it loves!
But instead of droplets, it gets a rave,
A party of dust, oh, how it misbehaves!

So here's a lesson from this hardy chap,
Patience is key—now take a nap!
When life throws sand, just take it in stride,
And laugh at the sun, oh, what a ride!

Veils of Verity

Wearing green armor, a quirky knight,
Stands in the garden, a marvelous sight.
With a grin that's prickly and oddly bright,
It jests about water, 'Don't forget to light!'

Hiding secrets beneath its green hue,
It whispers sly jokes, only to you.
"I'm drought-proof," it chuckles, with all of its pride,
"Why rush for water? I'm taken for a ride!"

It watches the world through a wink and a sigh,
"Life's just a game, come give it a try!
When friends start to worry and frown in despair,
Just shrug and keep smiling, this is how we care."

So raise up a glass to this spiny old sage,
With humor and patience, it owns the stage.
In a world full of hurry, it takes a slow pace,
And teaches us laughter in this wild race!

From the Ashes of Austerity

In a dustbowl of dreams, it found its place,
Waving its spikes with a comical grace.
From barren beginnings, it sprouted anew,
With a quip and a quirk, who knew it could do?

Striking a pose in the midday heat,
It shakes off the dust with joyous defeat.
"Hard times can't stop me!" it shouts with glee,
"For I am the boss of total esprit!"

As storms come and go, with a flick and a twist,
It chuckles aloud, "I've a long wait list!
Don't bother with gloom, raise your chin to the sky,
Just watch me, dear friends, as I bloom—oh my!"

A cheer for resilience, a toast to the jest,
In troubles of life, it's laughter we test.
So when times are tough, just take a good look,
At the one who thrives—be the joyful book!

Cradled in Courage

In a corner of chaos, it stands so bold,
With patience as armor, not easily sold.
It chuckles and sways, defying each storm,
Who knew that stubbornness could be so warm?

With wisdom like rings on a well-weathered tree,
It shares good advice, "Come laugh with me!"
When the world tries to poke and prod, oh what glee,
"I simply grow stronger, just you wait and see!"

When friends are down, it throws a wonky dance,
With wiggles and wobbles, it takes its stance.
With jokes on its thorns and joy in its heart,
Who needs a spa day when laughter's an art?

So here's to the soul that stands through it all,
With laughter and love, it'll never fall.
Be brave like the spines that dare to dream wide,
For courage is laughter, it's all a joyride!

The Color of Steadfastness

In the desert where it's dry, fast
A prickly friend with patience will last.
Standing tall through the heat and the sun,
Spinning tales of endurance, oh what fun!

Dressed in green, with spikes for attire,
A humorous figure, igniting our fire.
Each poke a reminder, don't move too fast,
Life's best moments are meant to last.

Roots grip the ground, never in a rush,
Calmly sipping water, amidst the hush.
Laughing at storms, with a cheeky grin,
Teaching the world, patience is a win!

So here's to that sprout, forever it waits,
Sending joy with its funny updates.
When life's a tumble and spirits may fall,
Remember this jester, standing so tall!

Remnants of Resilience

Amidst the chaos, there shines a spark,
A green little warrior lives in the dark.
With a laugh and a poke, it lifts heavy hearts,
Showing us all, tenderness imparts.

Resilience wrapped in a thorny disguise,
When the world gets rough, it simply complies.
With a wit that tickles, but armor so tough,
Teaching the lesson, 'life is always rough.'

Jokes from the desert, as dust starts to rise,
A quirky reminder, we all must realize.
Through laughter and pricks, we learn to stand tall,
Facing life's challenges, we can conquer all.

So let's raise a toast to our prickly friend,
With every endeavor, may patience blend.
In the game of life, its humor shines bright,
Building our spirits with sheer delight!

Blooming in a Sea of Suffering

In a garden of trouble, it plants its feet,
A cheerful green figure, brings joy bittersweet.
Waving its arms in the air with delight,
Sprouting laughter, making wrongs feel right.

While others may wilt in the heat of the day,
It stands there laughing, come what may.
A bloom with a punchline, humor so bright,
Showing us joy can outshine the night.

Amidst all the chaos, it holds its own show,
Bristling with jokes, putting on quite a glow.
Even when hairpin turns make us stray,
This jester of joy cheers us on our way.

So here's to the blooms in the toughest of trails,
With the spirit of laughter, it happily sails.
In every heartache, it plants seeds of cheer,
A master of funny, ever sincere!

The Beauty of Waiting

In a world that rushes, it takes its sweet time,
A plucky little sage, with rhythm and rhyme.
Turning each moment into a chuckle or two,
While waiting for blooms, it knows what to do.

With its thorns as the punchlines and wisdom so bright,
It laughs at the hurry, under moonlight.
Patience is an art, a canvas well drawn,
In this gallery of laughter, it graciously yawns.

While others grow restless, it dances in glee,
Sipping the sunlight like sweet herbal tea.
Keeping its cool in the face of impatience,
Its beauty lies deeply in joyful perseverance.

So next time you're stuck in a queue or a line,
Remember the beauty of taking your time.
With humor as armor, let the minutes flow,
For waiting's a skill to cherish and glow!

The Warrior's Green

In the land where the sun loves to bake,
A warrior grows for his own belly's sake.
With spikes on his armor, he struts so proud,
Filling the air with his spiky cloud.

When rain drops fall, he dances with glee,
Like a knight in a dream, just wait and see.
His friends call him 'Needles,' so brave and spry,
But really, it's just the way he gets dry.

In battle with thirst, he holds his ground,
While sipping from dew, he wears a crown.
His foes, they can't touch him; they're too wet to fight,
For he's made from sunshine and sheer delight.

So here's to the green warrior we adore,
In his prickly armor, he always wants more.
With humor so sharp and a heart so true,
He teaches us all to thistle right through.

A Life Unfazed

In the desert heat where nothing insists,
Lives a little green fellow, who hardly exists.
With arms wide open, he waves to the wind,
Saying, 'I'm fine, just don't let it grin!'

His pals all around are a bit less refined,
But they laugh and they cheer, 'We've been well defined!'

They soak up the sun and they never complain,
Just bask in the warmth like they're on a plane.

When clouds roll in, oh, how they all shriek,
'Hide your water stash, it's the end of the week!'
Yet a sprinkle or two just makes them more bold,
In the daylight parade, the story's retold!

So here's to the life that refuses to fade,
With roots deep in dirt, it's a grand escapade.
No worries about what the neighbors might say,
He'll just find a joke, and then laugh all day!

Tales from the Cactus Patch

Gather 'round friends for some tales from the patch,
Where the green ones tell stories without any scratch.
With each little spore, they spin tales that shine,
About the wild winds and the sweet desert wine.

One sprout told of a lizard, all decked out in green,
Who thought he could dance, but just made a scene.
He slipped on a pebble, fell flat on his face,
Yet jumped up with style, and resumed his grace.

Another spoke proudly of the sun's wicked game,
How it winked down low and called every name.
Yet our pals waved back, 'We're not shy, oh no!
With our thick, spiky skin, we'll just let it glow!'

So laughter rings out in the prickly enclave,
In the realm of the tough, there's always a wave.
For in this patch's heart, it's not just the spines,
But the stories we share, with all of our vines.

The Unseen Frontier

Out in the wild, on an unseen frontier,
Live gnarled little soldiers, with nothing to fear.
They don't rise for battle; they smile instead,
And chuckle at storms as they dance in their bed.

With roots so deep, they plot their foray,
Like, 'What if a rabbit strolled by today?'
They'd just squirt out some water, a silly prank,
And laugh as it bounced off their large, green flank.

When sandstorms approach, they wave and they grin,
'You're late to the party; we were just about to begin!'
And when it departs, they sip on the breeze,
Sipping their sunshine, with spines at ease.

So here's to the unseen, where laughter runs free,
In a riot of colors and green jubilee.
With every bold brave tale under the blazing dome,
These spiky little warriors have truly found home.

Spines of Stillness

In the desert's wide embrace,
A prickly fella claims his space.
With arms so high and stance so bold,
He waits for rain, or so I'm told.

While others run in pouring rain,
He sits and smiles, and feels no pain.
Tickling the breeze with cheeky glee,
A master of tranquility.

Blooming Against the Odds

A single flower, bright and spry,
On spiky limbs that reach the sky.
Against the grit, he's quite the champ,
A tiny bloom, a desert stamp.

With sunshine's kiss and wind's embrace,
He takes a risk in this tough place.
Waving his colors, bright and bold,
A tale of courage to be told.

Sunlit Solitude

Up high on a sunny ledge,
He's found his peace, took the pledge.
No need for company or crowd,
In solitude, he feels quite proud.

With sunbeams dancing on his crown,
He sprinkles joy, won't wear a frown.
For laughing at those who rush and stew,
He's happy just to chill and chew.

Sagebrush Serenade

Among the sagebrush, he will sing,
In harmony with the buzzing thing.
A melody of prickled cheer,
His voice is strong, you'll want to hear.

With every note, he cracks a smile,
Making the desert life worthwhile.
And as the sun begins to fade,
He winks and plays a sunny serenade.

The Patient Watcher

In the sun, I sit so still,
Watching the world, an unwritten thrill.
While others rush with no time to spare,
I simply bloom, without a care.

The birds flit by, so quick and spry,
I raise my spines and ask them why.
They tease and taunt, they don't understand,
My secret of stillness isn't all that bland.

Napping in warmth, absorbing the rays,
The hustle fades in my sunny daze.
With a grin of green, I chuckle and sway,
Patience, my friend, is the brightest bouquet.

So let them hurry, let them despair,
I'll savor the silence, for life's unfair.
Here I thrive, without any rush,
I'm the patient watcher, in nature's hush.

Illuminated by Isolation

In my little pot, I stand alone,
Basking in glory while others moan.
The world gets loud, a chaotic spree,
Yet here in my corner, I'm wild and free.

Sunshine dances, a spotlight on me,
Dancing shadows, a comedy spree.
With my spiky humor, sharp and bright,
Isolation's a party, what a delight!

Friends come and go, but here I'll stay,
A light in the dark, in my green cabaret.
While they fret and fumble, fear the fall,
I bask in my solitude, I stand tall!

So raise a cup to the quiet ones,
Who laugh at the mayhem, with irritable puns.
Illuminated by love that feels quite strange,
My laughter echoes, sweet and deranged.

Solace in Silence

In the desert's hush, I find my song,
Where whispers of wind seem to belong.
Each grain of sand carries a sigh,
While I offer solace, under the sky.

Flowers bloom close, the odd ones out,
In the quiet, I'm sure there's no doubt.
I'll sip the stillness, it's rather fun,
As silly shadows dance in the sun.

My spikes keep secrets, oh what a jest,
In silence, I find my inner fest.
While others chatter, shouting in glee,
I chuckle and bask, just happy to be.

So here I'll sway, without any noise,
A strange little plant, with strange little joys.
Solace in silence, a way to unwind,
Life's not a race, it's peace that we find.

The Quiet Storm

In the still of the night, I quietly thrive,
Gathering strength, feeling so alive.
While raindrops patter in rhythm and rhyme,
I chuckle and dance, oh, isn't it prime?

A tempest in spines, a still little gale,
I watch the wild winds, while others just bail.
Under the radar, I wiggle and sway,
A secret storm brewing, in my own way.

The laughter of thunder, my favorite tune,
As I soak up the chaos, beneath the bright moon.
While most run for cover, I stand my ground,
A resilient delight, in silliness drowned.

So let the skies rumble, let the winds whirl,
In my dancing silence, there's magic to twirl.
The quiet storm laughs at the world outside,
With every gust, I wear my pride.

www.ingramcontent.com/pod-product-compliance
Lightning Source LLC
Chambersburg PA
CBHW072123070526
44585CB00016B/1537